918·1

Economically Developing Countries

Brazil

Anna Lewington and Edward Parker

Wayland

Economically Developing Countries

Bangladesh	**India**
Brazil	**Mexico**
China	**Nigeria**
Egypt	**Peru**
Ghana	**The Philippines**

Cover: Fruit for sale at Ver-O-Peso market in Belem.
Title page: The inhabitants of a flooded forest village in the Amazon peel manioc, their staple food and cash crop.
Contents page: The futuristic architecture of the city of Brasilia, in the geographical centre of Brazil.

The authors would like to thank the Living Earth Foundation
for their assistance with this book.

Series editor: Paul Mason
Editor: Polly Goodman
Photographer: Edward Parker
Series designer: Malcolm Walker

First published in 1995 by
Wayland (Publishers) Ltd
61 Western Road, Hove
East Sussex BN3 1JD, England

British Library Cataloguing in Publication Data
Lewington, Anna
    Brazil. – (Economically Developing Countries Series)
    I. Title II. Parker, Edward III. Series
    918.1

ISBN 0-7502-1003-6

Typeset by Kudos Design, England
Printed and bound by Lego, Italy

Contents

Introduction

'I live in a favela [slum] a long way from here, but I travel here because it is where the rich people come on Sundays.'
– accordion player, street market in the centre of Belem.

Brazil is a giant country. It is the fifth-largest country on earth – bigger than the USA (excluding Alaska) and twice as large as India. The country is so big that the whole of western Europe could fit inside it!

Brazil's huge population – the eighth largest in the world – is one of the most varied of any country: a mixture of Portuguese, African, Amerindian and many other nationalities, including German, Italian and Japanese. Brazilians in general are famous for their high spirits and spontaneity, and for their love of music and colourful festivals. However, people's standards of living vary enormously and most of the population is extremely poor.

Brazil is a country of great contrasts. Although it is now the tenth-richest country in the world, two-thirds of its people are estimated to live below the poverty line, and one-third are suffering from malnutrition. This makes Brazil the country with the biggest gap between rich and poor in the world.

The country is developing very fast and becoming an important industrial power. In fact, it is the most industrialized of all developing nations. But most people are not benefiting at all from this process, while a lucky few enjoy a standard of living that is as good or better than that of well-off Europeans or North Americans.

Brazil can boast some remarkable achievements in its economic development and trade. For example, it is the world's largest exporter of

Despite being one of the ten richest countries in the world, the majority of Brazil's population is poor.

The wealthy of Brazil have a lifestyle like that of the wealthy in Europe and the USA.

sugar and coffee, the second-largest producer of iron ore and tin, and the fifth-largest exporter of arms. It has the largest hydro-electric power station, the ninth-largest motor vehicle industry and a cattle herd smaller only than that of the USA. However, most Brazilians have no proper health care, and in 1993, 16 million children were estimated to be living rough on the streets of the biggest cities.

As Rio de Janeiro's famous carnival celebrations show, Brazilians are very good at putting on extravagant ceremonies and entertainments, despite widespread poverty. However, the country faces enormous social problems because of its uneven wealth. With abundant natural resources and so much potential for development, Brazil is sometimes referred to as the 'sleeping giant' of South America.

A vast country

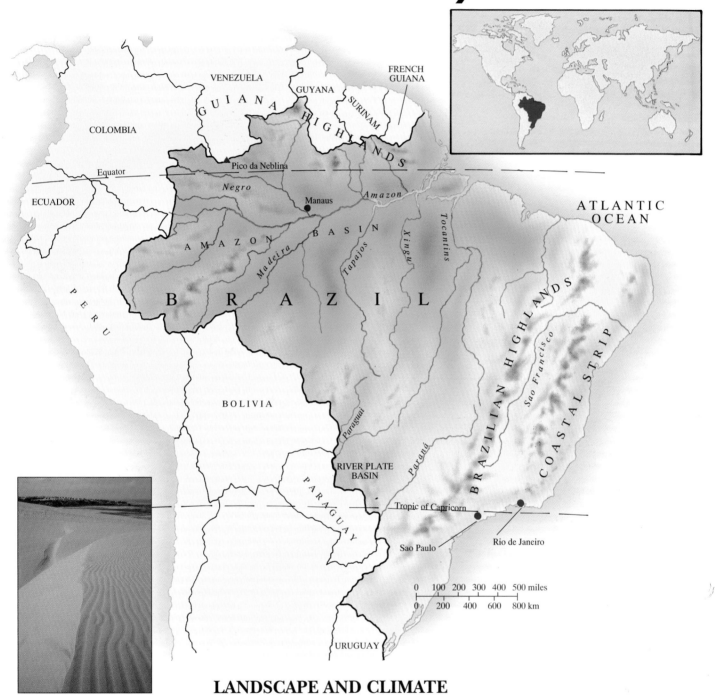

The sand dunes in the north-east reflect the periodic drought and tropical climate of the region.

LANDSCAPE AND CLIMATE

Brazil covers almost half the continent of South America and shares borders with all South America's countries except Chile and Ecuador. It also has the longest continuous coastline in the world. The country can be divided into five main topographical zones: the Amazon Basin; the River Plate Basin; the Guianan Highlands; the Brazilian Highlands, and the coastal strip.

6

The Amazon basin, in the north and west of the country, has few areas with altitudes higher than 250 m. Its climate is very constant, with temperatures around 27 °C, and high humidity. Rainforest vegetation, which is extremely varied, covers most of the region and large areas of the basin are flooded each year.

Several of the River Plate's tributaries, such as the Parana, drain towards the River Plate Basin in the south. The River Plate Basin is higher and cooler than the Amazon and is generally less heavily forested.

The Guiana Highlands are partly forested and partly arid. The area has wet and dry seasons and an annual average rainfall of 1,250 mm. Brazil's tallest mountain, Pico da Neblina, is found here, rising to 3,014 m (just under 10,000 ft).

The Brazilian Highlands, in the centre of the country, form a great tableland of between 300 – 900 m in height. The climate is 'altitude tropical', with an annual rainfall of less than 1,500 mm. The vegetation is mainly a lightly forested savanna known as *cerrado*, which gives way to dense forest towards the north and grassy prairies to the south.

The fertile land in Sao Paulo state is ideally suited to sugar cane, coffee and orange farming.

The coastal strip, a narrow belt of land running along the Atlantic coast of Brazil, has a tropical climate, with an average annual rainfall of 1,500 mm, and distinct wet and dry seasons. In Rio de Janeiro, temperatures can reach 40 °C in the summer but fall to 18 °C in winter. These seasonal variations become less pronounced as the coast extends further north.

One country, many peoples

The bulk of Brazil's population is found close to the Atlantic seaboard, while the interior is sparsely populated. Unlike all the other countries of South America, where Spanish is spoken, Brazil's language is Portuguese. But Portuguese is not the only language to be heard, because the population is made up of a fascinating blend of many nationalities – a mix of European, African and Amerindian.

FIRST PEOPLE; FIRST SETTLERS

The first people of Brazil were the Amerindians, who have lived on the continent for thousands of years. The original Amerindian population was possibly once as high as 10 million. However, their numbers were dramatically reduced in the early sixteenth century by disease and maltreatment as slaves and genocide.

Brazil's population is one of the most varied of any nation.

Today, about 200,000 Amerindians, belonging to around 200 different groups – or nations, as many prefer to be recognized – live in Brazil.

Brazil was colonized by Portugal in the late sixteenth century, and by the early nineteenth century 500,000 Portuguese had arrived. Many Portuguese men took Amerindian wives. Their children were the first of a new racial mixture which strongly influenced the language that developed: Brazilian Portuguese. There are many African words in this language, too, because soon after Brazil's discovery by Europeans, the first boat-loads of African slaves were brought to the north-east coast. Between 1532 and 1850, it is estimated that 5 million slaves were brought to Brazil from Guinea, Mozambique, Angola, the Congo and Benin, and each group brought its own distinct language and culture. The Candomblé religion, the samba dance and the spicy food eaten in the state of Bahia are just three aspects of African culture that have become part of modern Brazilian life.

These caboclo *children are child-minding for their elder relatives so that they can work. Like many* caboclos, *they live a day's journey from the nearest small town.*

POPULATION ORIGIN	
European	54%
Mixed	38%
African	6%
Japanese	1%
Amerindian and other	1%

The numbers of both Africans and Europeans are declining, while those of mixed race are growing.

IMMIGRATION

Like the USA, Brazil has many immigrants from other parts of the world who have come to settle there since the first settlers arrived. In the 1850s, after the slave trade was banned world-wide, the Brazilian government encouraged Europeans to come and live in Brazil. This was because workers were needed to replace the slaves. The first immigrants to arrive were mainly German and Swiss farmers, who settled in the temperate southern region of Brazil. Rather than mixing with the local people, they set up towns like Blumenau, which still has a distinctly Germanic feel. Around 200,000 Germans arrived in all.

Between 1884 and 1904, 1.4 million Italians arrived. Some settled around Sao Paulo to work on newly established coffee plantations, while others settled still further south to grow cereal crops and grapes. Others joined the growing urban workforce, and within two generations many were members of the powerful elite in Brazil. This influx of Italians was even greater than the flow of Portuguese (1.2 million) over the same period. Other nationalities to settle included 580,000 Spanish and 110,000 Russians, while another half a million came from European countries as varied as Greece, Poland and Lithuania. A large number of immigrants from Turkey, Syria and the Lebanon also live in Brazil.

The strong Germanic influence in the town of Blumenau, in southern Brazil, shows itself in the architecture of the town.

In 1908, the first of some 250,000 Japanese settled in Brazil. Most of their descendants now live in Sao Paulo, in the Japanese quarter called Liberdade. The Japanese have kept much of their culture intact and are the most prosperous of all Brazil's ethnic groups.

THE MELTING POT

Because there is such a mixture of nationalities in Brazil and the population is still changing, some refer to the country as a 'melting pot'. However, racial discrimination does exist. The constitution and laws of Brazil prohibit this, but black people are still barred from some restaurants and bars. Brazil has no black cabinet ministers or diplomats, and few leaders of corporations or powerful businesses are black. Amerindians are even worse off. Many Brazilians who live in cities, as well as government officials, have their own idea of Brazil as a modern industrial country, and would rather the Amerindians dressed and behaved in a conventional Western fashion. Most Amerindians are still struggling to get their basic human rights respected and to be allowed to live as they wish on their traditional lands.

When the Second World War ended in 1945, seven out of every ten people lived and worked in the countryside. Today, seven out of ten people live and work in cities, and the majority live close to the Atlantic coast. In fact, 40 per cent of Brazil's total population live in a strip of land that is only 100 km wide, which covers only 8 per cent of the country.

Amerindians in the Amazon peel manioc, a root vegetable that can be ground up into flour and made into bread.

The development of Brazil

As much as a quarter of Rio de Janeiro's population live in favelas like this one.

One of the most noticeable things about Brazil today is that its development has been very uneven. Millions of people live in *favelas* (slums), with no running water or electricity in their homes, access to little or no health care, and not enough to eat. Sometimes, only a few metres away, elegant apartments with private swimming pools, overlook the *favelas*. In such a rich nation, why does such inequality still exist? Many of the reasons lie in Brazil's history.

THE COLONIAL ERA

Although there is evidence that Phoenician sailors had reached the coast of Brazil several centuries earlier, Pedro Alvarez Cabral is credited with the 'discovery' of Brazil on 22 April 1500. He was trying to reach India via the newly discovered Cape of Good Hope, off the southern tip of South Africa, but his ship was blown off course.

For the next thirty years, a steady flow of small French and Portuguese ships sailed to Brazil in search of a valuable timber called pau-brazil, which produced a red dye. These trees, which gave Brazil its name, grew in a region inhabited by large groups of Amerindians, who bartered the logs for metal tools and other European goods. However, this situation did not last long and by the 1540s, the Portuguese had established a colony. The north-east

Brazil still depends on sugar produced by poorly paid workers on the plantations.

of Brazil proved to be an ideal environment for sugar plantations and the local Amerindians were soon forced into slavery. When they fled or died because of the dreadful treatment they received, they were replaced by slaves brought from Africa.

By the beginning of the eighteenth century, explorations into the interior of Brazil had led to the discovery of what was then the greatest gold mine in the world, at Minas Gerais. Between 1735 and 1754, an average of 14,500 kg of gold was shipped to Portugal each year.

After becoming independent in 1822, Brazil's economy continued to depend on the exploitation of poorly paid workers involved in mining and new forms of agriculture such as cattle ranching, cotton and coffee cultivation, and the collection of rubber. In the late nineteenth and early twentieth centuries, the huge world demand for rubber for car tyres caused a migration of people into the interior of the Amazon rainforest. Men and women worked in terrible conditions to collect what had become a valuable raw material. The 'rubber boom', as it was known, continued until 1911 and brought great wealth to the Amazonian cities of Belem and Manaus, but this wealth was unevenly distributed.

13

ECONOMIC INDICATORS 1993/4

Gross Domestic Product[1]
(size of the economy):   US$456 billion
Main Sectors of the Economy[2]:
       Manufacturing   25.0%
       Agriculture   10.8%
       Construction   7.1%
       Commerce   7.1%
       Mining   1.7%
Exports[1]:   US$41.3 billion
Imports[1]:   US$27.6 billion
Total External Debt: US$149 billion
Per Capita Income: US$3,150
(per year)   (UK equivalent: $16,530)

Sources: [1]Brazilian Ministry of Industry, Commerce
& Tourism, August 1994 [2]Economist Intelligence
Unit, Country Profile 1993/4

THE MODERNIZATION OF BRAZIL

Until the Second World War, Brazil had imported most of the manufactured goods it needed. But many of these supplies were cut off by the war, so Brazil had to develop new industries. The process of industrialization began in earnest with the election of President Juscelino Kubitschek. On taking office in 1955, Kubitschek promised 'fifty years progress in five'. He was the first president to make the growth of Brazil's economy his main objective, and he used government funds and money from abroad to invest in its development.

Large sums of money, for example, were spent on roads and hydroelectric schemes, and businesspeople were

The south-east of Brazil became industrialized at an incredible rate after the Second World War. This region now has an economy larger than any other South American country.

President Kubitschek (1955-61) was an important influence on Brazil's economic development.

encouraged to invest money in new enterprises in exchange for paying less tax. Foreign car manufacturers were invited to build factories in Brazil. All of this led to an explosion of industrialization. Between 1970 and 1974, Brazil enjoyed an economic growth rate of over 10 per cent a year, and until the 1980s, the average annual rate of growth was 8.9 per cent, which was still very high.

DEBT CRISIS

In 1982, Mexico decided that it could no longer afford to pay back its loans from abroad. This began the 'Latin American debt crisis' and stopped loans for development being made to Brazil. Brazil had to earn an extra $6 billion a year to try and pay back some of its debt, and the

---

SOCIAL INDICATORS

Income Distribution[1]:
>Wealthiest 20% earn around 65% of national income
>
>Poorest 20% earn less than 3%
>
>(this is the most extreme income inequality that has been measured by the World Bank)

Life Expectancy: 66 years overall[2]
>55 years in the north-east[3]
>
>(UK equivalent = 76 years)[2]

Infant Mortality[2] : 0–1 year: 60 per 1,000 (UK 8 per 1,000)
>1–4 years: 83 per 1,000 (UK 9 per 1,000)

Literacy[2]: 83% male
>80% female
>
>(UK equivalent 95%+)

Population per Doctor[4]: 1,080 (UK equivalent 870)

Percentage of Population under 20 years old: 45%
>(UK equivalent 26%) (24% are under 9)

Standard of Living[3]: Over 50% of homes have no electric lights,
>71% of homes have no running water, 79% have no fridge.

[1] A Survey of Brazil, (*The Economist*, 1991) [2] *Save the Children Country Report* (July 1992) [3] *Reforma ou Caos* 1992 [4] *Brazil: A Mask Called Progress* by Neil MacDonald (Oxfam, 1991)

---

government was forced to sharply reduce public spending. Brazil's poor suffered greatly as wages fell, prices soared and health standards deteriorated.

As the crisis got worse, the military handed back power to a civilian government after twenty-one years in control. Jose Sarney became president in March 1985 and tried to reduce inflation and boost growth. However, by the time President Collor became president in 1990, inflation was at 4,853 per cent a year (equivalent to about 14 per cent a month).

President Collor resigned in 1992 after being accused of corruption, and Itamar Franco became president. In June 1994, inflation reached a peak of nearly 50 per cent a month, but a dramatic change followed. In July, Finance Minister Fernando Enrique Cardoso – who later won the presidential elections in October – introduced a new currency, the Real, and a new plan to bring down inflation. By November 1994, it was down to less than 2 per cent a month. Brazilians hope that at last things will improve.

STREET CHILDREN

On Friday 23 January 1993, about fifty children were sleeping rough beside the Candelaria Church in Rio de Janeiro when a group of hooded gunmen started shooting them. Among the seven boys who died were Paulo Roberto de Oliveira, aged 11, and Marcelo Candido de Jesus, aged 14.

Three military policemen were put in custody charged with the killings, but it is very unusual for anyone to be punished for this kind of crime.

Death squads, often made up of off-duty policemen, are paid by local businesspeople to 'clean up' their neighbourhoods of robbers, petty thieves and children who live on the streets because their parents are too poor to look after them.

In the first six months of 1993, 328 children had been killed in Rio de Janeiro alone. The National Street Children's Movement has been set up to defend children's rights in Brazil.

Street children in Salvador looking through rubbish.

RICH NATION, POOR PEOPLE

The inequalities of colonial times still exist in Brazil. Today there are 'two Brazils' – one rich, one poor – with the wealth concentrated in the hands of a few people and the costs borne by the poor and the natural environment. Currently, the combined earnings of the top 1 per cent of Brazilian society are larger than those of the poorest 50 per cent, and 4.5 per cent of the population own 81 per cent of the land. Agricultural growth has risen faster than the population in the last thirty years. But agricultural land has been used to produce ever-greater quantities of export crops, like sugar, oranges and soya, rather than to grow the staple foods like beans (*feijao*) that Brazilians eat.

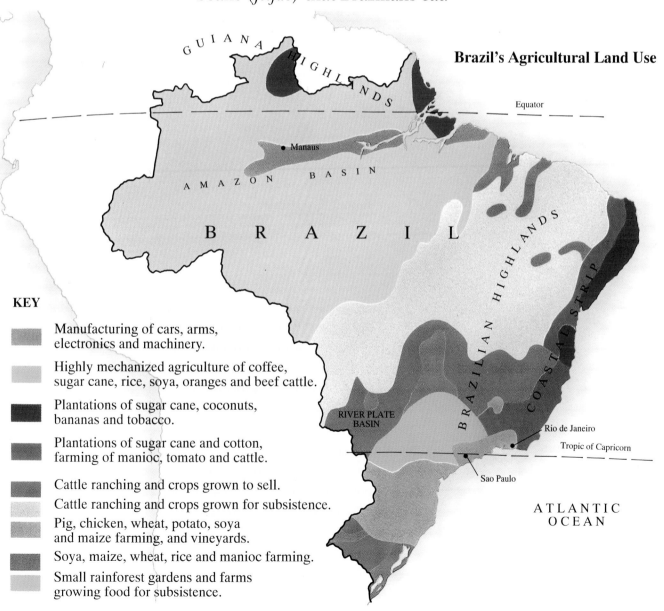

Brazil's Agricultural Land Use

KEY

- Manufacturing of cars, arms, electronics and machinery.
- Highly mechanized agriculture of coffee, sugar cane, rice, soya, oranges and beef cattle.
- Plantations of sugar cane, coconuts, bananas and tobacco.
- Plantations of sugar cane and cotton, farming of manioc, tomato and cattle.
- Cattle ranching and crops grown to sell.
- Cattle ranching and crops grown for subsistence.
- Pig, chicken, wheat, potato, soya and maize farming, and vineyards.
- Soya, maize, wheat, rice and manioc farming.
- Small rainforest gardens and farms growing food for subsistence.

The north-east: soul of Brazil

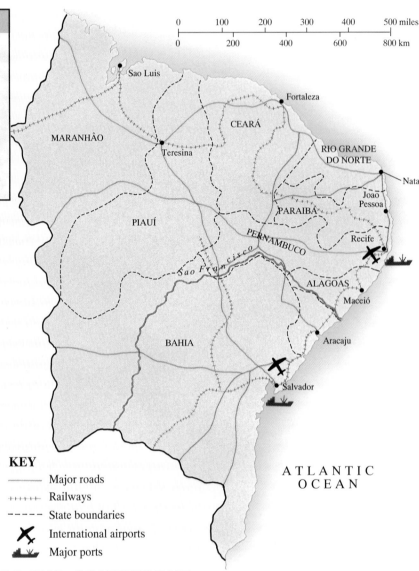

KEY

—— Major roads

++++++ Railways

- - - - State boundaries

✈ International airports

⚓ Major ports

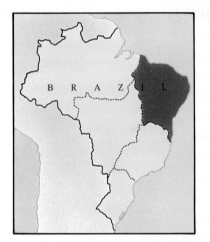

The colonial buildings of Olinda represent the former wealth from sugar plantations.

SOCIAL CONDITIONS: BRAZIL'S POOREST REGION

To people in the south and south-east of Brazil, the north-east is like another country and an embarrassment to the nation. After a brief period of wealth in the early colonial era, when it was the first area to be colonized by the Europeans, the north-east has been in a long decline. It is now the poorest region. However, the colourful traditions and music associated with its large black population have helped to earn the north-east its name, 'the soul of Brazil'.

18

A Bahian woman in traditional costume.

Today, the majority of the population has an appalling standard of living. About 86 per cent of the children in the north-east suffer from malnutrition of some sort, and the region also has the highest incidence of infectious diseases. Out of every 1,000 children born, 100 die at birth, compared to a national average of 61 per 1,000. Life expectancy is 55 years, as opposed to 65 years in the south, and 60 per cent of the region's work-force earns less than $1,000 per year. Many sugar-cane workers still earn the equivalent of only 30 pence a day. Nearly half the people cannot read or write, in comparison with just 17 per cent in the south-east.

THE ECONOMY:
NEW HOPE FROM TOURISM AND OIL

From colonial times right up until today, the north-east's economy has been based mainly on inefficient agriculture and related processing industries. Although the south-east became rapidly industrialized between 1940 and 1980, very little money was invested in the north-east, and it has relied on government support.

The 'Sons of Gandhi' are a Candomblé religious group. Candomblé religions include elements of West African and Catholic religion in their beliefs.

The Rise and Fall of Sugar

For the first two centuries of Portuguese colonization, great fortunes were made by sugar estate owners. These fortunes declined in the second half of the seventeenth century because Europe cultivated its own sugar from sugar beet, a different sugar-producing plant. But sugar cane made a strong comeback in the 1970s as the source of a fuel on which vehicles could be run. Oil had become so expensive that it was more economical to convert vehicles to run on sugar-cane alcohol (ethanol).

Today, all petroleum used for vehicles in Brazil has to have a 20 per cent ethanol content.

Despite the revival of fortunes in the sugar-cane industry, social conditions have not improved much for the workers.

Maria José Trajano da Silva is a sugar-cane worker in the state of Paraiba. She works from 5.00 am until 5.00 pm, with a two-hour break in the middle of the day. Her pay amounts to the equivalent of £1.80 a week. Men get the equivalent of about £2.40

Sugar-cane alcohol is used as an alternative to petrol in Brazil in an attempt to reduce the quantity of oil imported.

However, new hope for the economy has come from the development of offshore oil fields and the establishment of refineries. The state of Bahia now supplies 80 per cent of Brazil's petroleum requirements. With thousands of kilometres of tropical beaches, the north-east is also

Workers on the sugar plantations of the north-east are very poorly paid, earning sometimes less than the equivalent of 50 pence per day. Brazil is the largest exporter of sugar in the world.

for exactly the same work of planting and weeding. It takes cane workers about two days to earn enough to buy a kilo of beans and three days to be able to buy two kilos of sugar or a bottle of cooking oil.

In 1990 there was a serious drought which meant that the plantations hired fewer workers because of the poor sugar crop. This made the situation even worse for the cane workers because most had no work, and their own small gardens produced little food. Poor farmers have been pushed on to land that is difficult to work because the sugar-cane plantations have taken over more and more of the best land.

'There is nothing. We are eating only manioc flour. There are no beans to buy now . . . I have four children. The hunger is tremendous. I go to work with only a cigarette. I don't eat.' – **Maria José Trajano da Silva, sugar-cane worker.**

promoting tourism to improve the economy. Irrigation schemes using water from the Sao Francisco river have enabled market gardens and orchards to be set up in the arid interior, and three-quarters of Brazil's total tobacco crop is grown in Bahia.

Although the droughts of the north-east have caused terrible hardship in the north-east, another frightening but less well-known factor has caused the death of hundreds of innocent people and the migration to other regions of thousands more. Since the early 1980s, powerful landowners have been forcing smallholders to abandon their land.

In Brazil, land means power. In the state of Maranhao, where many poor families fled years ago to escape the droughts further south in Ceará, land speculation and fear of agrarian reform (which would give land back to the smallholders) have prompted an epidemic of violence. Hired thugs have been burning farmers' homes, poisoning their crops and torturing and killing people. It is sometimes those in the highest positions, who should be able to stop the violence, who are believed to be secretly involved.

Smallholders like these are often at risk from large, powerful landowners, who use violence to try and force them off their land.

STAMPING OUT CORRUPTION IN CEARÁ

Ceará is a small state with a population of only 6.5 million. In 1986, the three most powerful people in the state disagreed on whom they should try to promote as state governor, and a little-known politician named Tasso Jereissati – whom none of them had promoted – won the election.

Jereissati immediately set out to stop corruption and improve conditions for the poor. Schools and hospitals were falling apart and the infant death rate was the highest in Brazil. He found that thousands of people were paid for jobs they did not do, and that some civil servants were paid ten salaries. Jereissati fired thousands of state employees, started to collect tax properly and redirected the money to repair schools, build roads and employ more doctors. This example shows that the economy and social conditions can improve quickly when there is good state government.

Fishing boats called jangadas, *similar to those seen by the first Portuguese sailors in 1530, are still used for ocean fishing in the north-east.*

23

The south-east: economic powerhouse

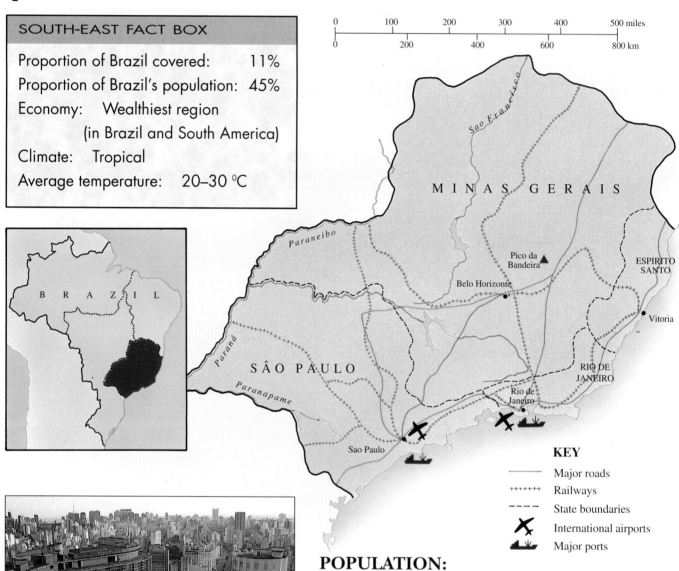

SOUTH-EAST FACT BOX

Proportion of Brazil covered: 11%
Proportion of Brazil's population: 45%
Economy: Wealthiest region
           (in Brazil and South America)
Climate: Tropical
Average temperature: 20–30 ℃

KEY
— Major roads
+++++++ Railways
– – – State boundaries
✕ International airports
⚓ Major ports

The centre of São Paulo appears much like any other large city in the world.

POPULATION: INTERNATIONAL IMMIGRATION

The population of the south-east is enormous. Nearly half of the total inhabitants of Brazil are squeezed into its four states. The main cultural influence in the south-east today has come from the descendants of European, Asian and Middle-Eastern immigrants.

24

SOCIAL CONDITIONS:
SLUMS AND WEALTHY SUBURBS

As in other parts of Brazil, social conditions vary enormously. But it is in the south-east that the gap between rich and poor is most obvious. For example, wealthy homes in the fashionable suburb of Morumbi, in São Paulo, may have ten to fifteen servants and an expensive limousine as the family car. In contrast, the *favela* (slum) called Rocinha, in Rio de Janeiro, has at least 60,000 people living in shacks, crammed on to one small hill. There is no sewage system and many *favelas* have no running water. There are no formal education or health care facilities for over 1 million people who live in the slums of Rio.

Las Clinicas Hospital

The Las Clinicas hospital in São Paulo is the largest public hospital complex in South America. It has a budget of $20 million per month, and in 1993 it treated 864,198 patients. The hospital has the very latest equipment, and its pioneering research attracts specialists from around the world.

An angioplasty (heart operation) at Las Clinicas hospital is monitored on the latest computerized equipment.

'*This is a first-world hospital.*'
– **the Director of Nuclear Radiotherapy.**

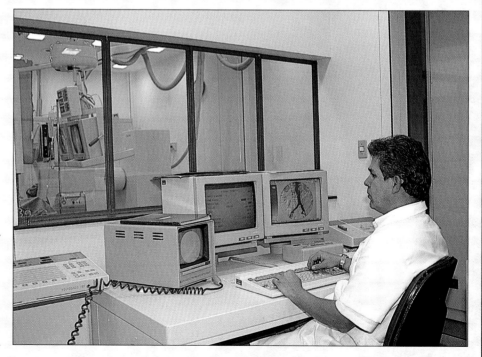

One of Brazil's most famous attractions is its carnival, celebrated each year during the week before Lent. Although *Carnaval*, as it is known, is celebrated throughout Brazil, the festivities in Rio have become world famous.

Today's Rio Carnival has three main parts: riotous street events; balls, organized by traditional clubs; and the samba parade. The street celebrations attract thousands of people, in extravagant fancy dress, intent on enjoying themselves. Contests for the best costume are held at several of the balls. But the most colourful event, and the centrepiece of the carnival, is the samba school parade. Musicians and dancers from fourteen different samba schools parade through the city on huge, decorated floats. Each year, a winning school is chosen by judges, who award points for the best costumes and overall effect.

The state of São Paulo has 150 million orange trees and Brazil is the largest exporter of oranges in the world.

ECONOMY: ECONOMIC POWERHOUSE

The south-east is Brazil's wealthiest region. At first, the fortunes made from cotton and coffee in this region provided the investment capital which boosted Brazil's extraordinary economic growth at the end of the nineteenth and the beginning of the twentieth centuries.

Today, the south continues to have a large number of major economic activities. Agriculture is still very important. For example, Brazil is now the world's largest exporter of oranges, and supplies 85 per cent of the world's orange juice – all produced in this region. There are about 150 million orange trees in the state of São Paulo alone. The hilly, fertile land of the south-east has also enabled Brazil

The *Favelas*

Despite the prosperity of the south-east, there are thousands of *favelas*, or slums, scattered across the region. Rio de Janeiro has almost 500 of its own, and they are home to more than a quarter of the city's population.

Maria Aparecida lives in a *favela* in Bauru, a city in the heart of Sao Paulo state. She has six children, four of whom she adopted because their parents couldn't afford to look after them. She gets some help with clothes from a local charity but otherwise earns what she can washing clothes.

Favelas have become the last resort for millions of poor people who have been forced to move to the big cities in search of work. The high price of houses and the low-paid jobs mean that finding proper accommodation is extremely difficult.

Maria Aparecida de Cavalho does her laundry in the favela *that she lives in.*

'*Life is very hard. I live in a small, two-room house with my six children. It has no electricity and there are only two sinks with running water for everyone in the favela.*'
– Maria Aparecida, Bauru.

to become the biggest producer of coffee. In addition to this, industrial centres manufacture huge numbers of cars, arms, electronic goods, pieces of machinery and tools, and the rivers produce an enormous quantity of hydroelectric power. A vast service sector has grown up, and a major tourist industry has also developed.

THE MOTOR INDUSTRY: MULTINATIONALS AND UNIONS

The Brazilian motor industry began in the late 1950s. The government was trying to reduce imports, so multinational car manufacturers were invited to invest in Brazilian industry. The new companies were to become the main source of long-term investment in industry. Originally, vehicles were made for use in Brazil alone, but increasing numbers are being exported. In 1992, Brazil produced 1,069,218 vehicles, of which approximately one-third were exported.

Above *Brazil's motor industry produces over a million vehicles a year, ranging from Mercedes buses to the latest models from General Motors.*

The industrialization of Brazil has led to serious environmental problems. Cubatao's industrial area is reputed to be one of the most polluted places on earth and the health of local children in particular has been seriously affected.

During the 1960s and 1970s, multinationals such as Ford, General Motors, Volkswagen, Fiat, Saab-Scania, Volvo and Mercedes Benz poured millions of dollars into Brazil, creating the largest motor industry of any developing nation, and the ninth-largest in the world. Concentrated in São Paulo, the rise of the motor industry created thousands of skilled jobs, a Brazilian-owned parts industry and a ready market for Brazil's steel. By the end of 1987, multinational investment and reinvestment stood at $23 billion and car manufacturers employed 18.5 per cent of the work force.

Many poor people were inspired by the car workers of São Paulo when, in 1978, they challenged the military government. There were then 38,000 workers at Volkswagen alone, and 25,000 at Ford. There were also 210,000 metal workers in the industrial belt around São Paulo. On 12 May 1978, a strike broke out at the Saab-Scania plant, for higher wages and protection from the high inflation rates. The strike quickly spread through the state of São Paulo, eventually involving nearly half a million workers. The car and metal workers won their strike, but this was not all they achieved. An important union leader emerged named Luis Inacio da Silva (Lula), who was only narrowly defeated in the 1990 elections. He ran for the presidency again in October 1994 but was narrowly beaten by Fernando Enrique Cardoso of the P.S.D.B. party.

To many poor people, who are working for improvements in their communities, 1978 was the year when things began to change.

The north: Amazon rainforest

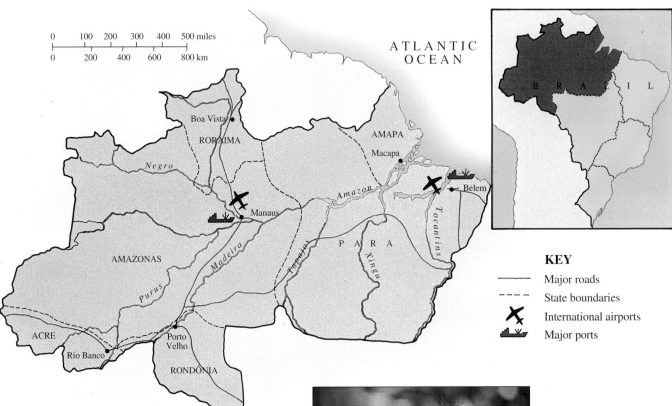

ATLANTIC OCEAN

0 100 200 300 400 500 miles
0   200   400   600   800 km

Boa Vista
RORAIMA
AMAPA
Macapa
Negro
AMAZONAS
Amazon
PARA
Tocantins
Manaus
Madeira
Purus
Xingu
Tapajos
ACRE
Porto Velho
Rio Banco
RONDÔNIA
Belem

B R A Z I L

KEY
—— Major roads
---- State boundaries
✈ International airports
🚢 Major ports

THE NORTH FACT BOX

Area covered: 4,840,000 km²

Proportion of Brazil covered: 42%
(biggest region)

Proportion of Brazil's population: 8%

Economy: Based on the natural
resources of iron ore, bauxite
(aluminium ore), timber, palm fruits,
Brazil nuts, gold and diamonds.

Climate: Equatorial. Humid.

Average temperature: 25–30 °C
all year round

Average annual rainfall: 2,500 mm
(heavy)

The Amazon rainforest contains a bewildering number and variety of plant and animal species such as this endangered uakari monkey.

30

Rubens, a waiter in a top hotel in Belem.

POPULATION – AMERINDIANS, CABOCLOS AND SETTLERS

The majority of Brazil's Amerindians live in the Amazon region. Many peoples have been reduced to only a handful of individuals, but a few are still relatively numerous. The Tukano nation, for example, number about 18,000 and the Brazilian Yanoamö about 8,000–9,000.

As well as Amerindians, there are many thousands of *caboclos*. These are the descendants of Amerindians and Europeans who have settled along the banks of the 'whitewater' rivers, where vast Amerindian communities like the Omaguas used to live. They live simply, hunting and gathering forest products such as fish, fruits and Brazil nuts, which they also sell to traders.

More numerous than both these groups are the hundreds of thousands of settlers, or colonists, who have arrived from other parts of Brazil in recent years in search of a better life, both in the forest and in the cities.

SOCIAL CONDITIONS – GENERALLY POOR

In the Amazon interior and in the cities, the majority of people are very poor. Rubens, a waiter in one of the top hotels in Belem, gets up at 5 am to travel from a poor suburb into town. Like many people, Rubens has little access to proper health care and his rheumatism sometimes makes it difficult for him to work.

There are some very serious diseases in the Amazon region, including yellow fever and malaria (carried by mosquitoes), cholera, typhus, tuberculosis, African river blindness and rabies. Amerindians, in particular, suffer greatly from these non-native diseases.

31

A family in a remote part of the Amazon sifts manioc (cassava) flour on to a large iron pan to toast it.

Although school is free, many children have no schools in their area, or their families are so poor that they need the children to work.

ECONOMY – MASSIVE NATURAL RESOURCES

Amerindians have always used and traded rainforest products with little disturbance to the forest. Tens of thousands of people continue to depend directly on the forest today.

Exporting Brazil Nuts

Mauro Mutran is one of the main exporters of brazil nuts in Brazil. He buys the nuts from Amerindians and *caboclos*, who gather them by hand from the rainforest. Britain is the biggest importer of brazil nuts in Europe, but recently prices have fallen dramatically.

'The income of thousands of people is now at risk because it's becoming uneconomic to deal in brazil nuts. This means that more forest will probably be destroyed and used for other purposes.' – Mauro Mutran, brazil nut exporter.

Brazil is extremely rich in mineral resources. As well as reserves of gold in the Amazon region, there are important deposits of bauxite, from which aluminium is extracted, and in 1991, Brazil was the world's leading producer of cassiterite, the source of tin.

In 1967, the largest-known iron-ore deposit in the world was discovered in the Serra dos Carajas mountains in the state of Pará. An estimated 18 billion tonnes of iron ore exist there – some 350 – 400 years' worth of reserves. However, this forms only the core of what has become an integrated development area. Grande Carajas, as it is known, also includes the mining of manganese, copper, bauxite, cassiterite and gold, as well as logging, charcoal production, iron and aluminium smelting and agro-industrial plantations covering 800,000 km²

of what was Amazonian forest. This represents an area bigger than France and Britain put together. The region is expected to earn more than $17 billion a year as the ore is destined for export. The European Community is the largest funder of the Carajas project and in return, has been promised 13.6 million tonnes of ore a year for fifteen years, at very low prices.

Above The north region has the world's largest reserves of both timber and iron ore.

In contrast, many of the large-scale economic activities in the Amazon cause extensive damage to the rainforest – for example much ranching, mining and logging.

Today, the Amazonian economy is still based on natural resources. The northern region has the world's largest deposits of iron ore and bauxite, and the largest timber reserves, as well as gold and diamonds. The major cities of the north are mainly involved in processing raw products from the region, such as palm fruits, brazil nuts and timber. Manaus is a collection and distribution centre for towns all along the Amazon River. It became a free-trade zone in 1967 and large quantities of electronic goods are also sold there.

Fishing is also important locally and fish is a major source of protein for Amazonian people.

Fruits From The Forest

Combu Island is situated on the River Guamá, only 3 km from the city of Belem. Orivaldo Quaresma lives on the island, where he collects the dark purple fruit from the *açai* palms to sell in the markets of Belem. These palms grow naturally in the forest and Orivaldo collects their fruit by climbing each tree and cutting off the stalks, which bear hundreds of berries.

Orivaldo earns a relatively good living by selling *açai* to people who make fruit juices and ice cream. He earns between $2,500 and $3,000 a year, some of which also comes from selling cocoa.

The lifestyle of the inhabitants of Combu island and their use of their natural resources have recently been the subject of much academic interest, because the people have been able to enjoy a relatively high standard of living without destroying their environment. Belem's famous Emilio Goeldi Museum has been co-ordinating this research.

'Climbing açai *palm trees isn't easy, but the fruit from each tree is worth more money than you get labouring for a week in the city [Belem]. We also grow cacao trees in the forest which we sell in the season when there is no* açai *fruit.'* – **Orivaldo Quaresma,** açai ***fruit collector and seller, Combu Island.***

The collection of açai *palm fruit (detail inset) by people living in the rainforest provides an income whilst causing little disturbance to the forest.*

A young boy from Mamirana practises how to harpoon fish.

MERCURY POISONING

During the 1980s, thousands of people flooded into the Amazon rainforest in search of gold. The appalling conditions they worked in and the problems they were causing local Amerindians became famous in 1989, when it was revealed that about 45,000 garimpeiros, as the miners are called, had moved on to Yanoamö Amerindian land.

There may be half a million gold miners in the Amazon today, leading a nomadic lifestyle. As well as destroying river banks with high-pressure water hoses, they use mercury to separate the mud they sieve from the gold. Mercury is extremely poisonous. It is estimated that about 1,000 tonnes may be joining the network of Amazonian rivers each year and entering the food chain. Fish in one river in Rondonia were recently shown to have four times the World Health Organization's safety level of mercury. Large numbers of people who depend on the Amazonian fish are now at risk from mercury poisoning. The effects include irreversible damage to the nervous system.

Centre-west: the wild west

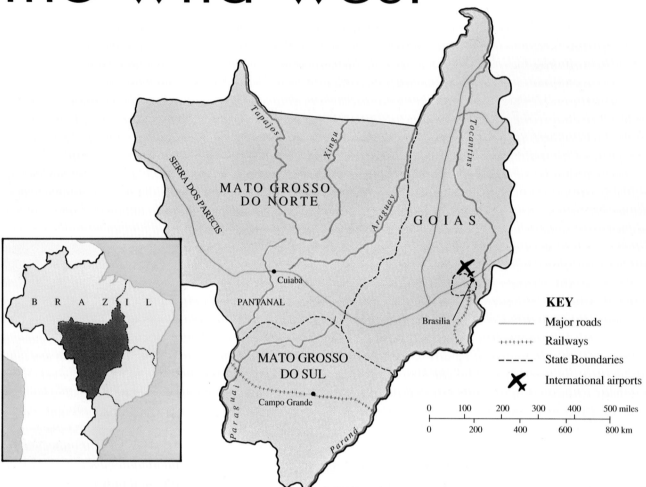

B R A Z I L

MATO GROSSO
DO NORTE

SIERRA DOS PARECIS

Tapajos

Xingu

Araguay

Tocantins

G O I A S

Cuiaba

PANTANAL

Brasilia

MATO GROSSO
DO SUL

Paraguai

Campo Grande

Parana

KEY

— Major roads

+++++ Railways

- - - - State Boundaries

✗ International airports

0	100	200	300	400	500 miles

0	200	400	600	800 km

CENTRE-WEST FACT BOX

Proportion of Brazil covered: 21%
    (second-largest region)

Proportion of Brazil's population: 6.4%

Population: 9.4 million

Economy: Agriculture, ranching,
    mining and government
    service industries

Climate: Tropical. Cooler than north
    and north-east. Distinct wet
    and dry seasons.

Average annual rainfall: 1,500 mm

Many of the roads in the centre-west are still unpaved, although communications are now improving.

The Mato Grosso of western Brazil has been opened up to large-scale agriculture such as cattle ranching and the cultivation of soya beans over the last twenty years.

POPULATION: SPARSELY POPULATED

The centre-west was once home to a great number of Amerindian nations. It is still an important area for Brazil's remaining peoples, such as the Mehinaku, Suya, Juruna and others, who live in the Xingu National Park.

Until the beginning of the eighteenth century the area was largely uncolonized, but in 1719, a large deposit of gold was found near Cuiabá and the region's population grew rapidly. After this, immigration was encouraged by the government in order to relieve the pressure on land in other areas of Brazil. Today, there are about 100,000 new arrivals every year.

SOCIAL CONDITIONS: 'THE WILD WEST'

'A land without men for men without land' was how President Emilio Medici described the centre-west in the 1970s, in an effort to attract the poor from the over-populated south. It was promoted as the last frontier, where land was free and riches awaited the strong and brave. Sadly, this was a myth, and the thousands who arrive every year find that the best land is owned by large companies and wealthy families. These lands are often protected from squatters by pistoleiros, or hired gunmen. The centre-west is

The Pantanal is one of the world's great wilderness areas. Situated on Brazil's western frontier with Bolivia, it is a region of swamp the size of France and has a great density of wildlife. For Brazilians, the Pantanal is the country's major ecological attraction. Alligators, jaguars, deer, otters and monkeys can all be seen from tourist boats and the area has over 600 species of bird. It is also a haven for fish, and has some 350 species, including the enormous pintado fish, which can weigh up to 80 kg.

Surprisingly, people and cattle seem to co-exist with the wildlife with apparently few problems. Local farmers and the Brazilian Parks Authority protect the Pantanal jealously, but the poaching of cayman (alligator), ocelot and jaguar skins has become a serious problem.

A soap opera called *Pantanal*, which also features the wildlife of the region, recently became one of the most popular series on Brazilian television.

Above   The Pantanal is a vast swamp where man and nature appear to live relatively harmoniously.

popularly known as 'the wild west', and only in the last twenty years have paved roads been built in the region.

THE ECONOMY – COWBOYS AND MINERS

Settlers were first attracted to the region by the prospect of catching Amerindian slaves and of finding gold. Gold, and later diamonds found close to Cuiabá, provided the first economic base for the region.

Today, extensive agriculture based on maize, rice and soya-bean cultivation, and cattle ranching dominate the centre-west. It is also the location of the world's largest soya-bean farm. The undulating savanna is grazed by large herds of beef cattle, rounded up by gauchos, or cowboys. Mining, in particular for lead ore, and the logging of hardwoods are also important economic activities.

The Brazilian Government and all the Ministries have been located in the capital city of Brasilia since 1960, and the service industries that support the city are another important part of the economy.

BRASILIA

Brazilians were thinking of moving their capital to the centre of the country as early as the eighteenth century, but it was not until the election of Juscelino Kubitschek, in 1955, that the idea became a reality.

In less than four years a new city, Brasilia, had been built at the geographical heart of Brazil. This was an extraordinary feat as there were no roads or railways nearby and all the workers

and their supplies had to be flown in. The design of the city is like an aeroplane or bow and arrow, with the government buildings at the centre and two 'wings' of residential and business areas on either side. The main buildings were designed by the architect Oscar Niemeyer and the capital was inaugurated on 21 April 1960.

With its extraordinary design of buildings, Brasilia stands as a symbol of a new and dynamic Brazil, but the design of the city makes life difficult for many of its people. For example, the design failed to make any allowances for future growth. Originally planned to have a population of 500,000 by the year 2000, it already has a total population of 1.598 million. The temporary settlements on the outskirts which were designed to be used only by construction workers during the building of the city, are now home to the poor people who work in low-paid jobs in the centre. The centre of Brasilia is spacious and grassy but has been designed for cars rather than pedestrians.

Above Brasilia's cathedral was designed by architect Oscar Niemeyer.

Below Poor workers in Brasilia live on rough land, or in one of the favelas that surround the city.

The south: land of four seasons

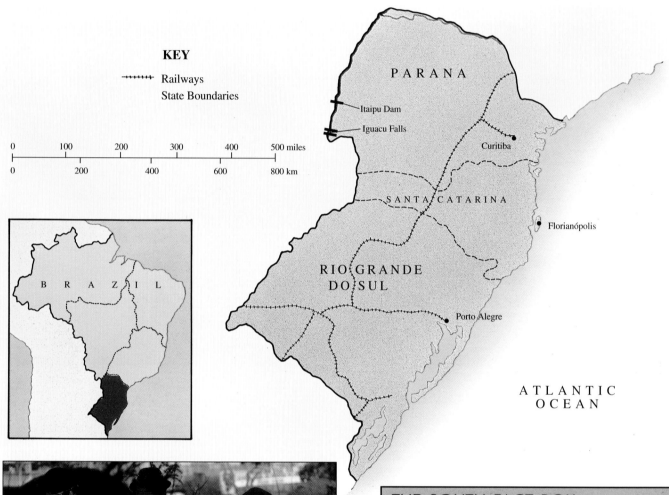

KEY

-++++- Railways

State Boundaries

P A R A N A

Itaipu Dam
Iguacu Falls
Curitiba

S A N T A C A T A R I N A

Florianópolis

RIO GRANDE
DO SUL

Porto Alegre

A T L A N T I C
O C E A N

B R A Z I L

Descendants of Italian immigrants wrapped in warm clothes on a frosty morning in Caxias do Sul.

THE SOUTH FACT BOX

Proportion of Brazil covered: 7%
(smallest region)

Proportion of Brazil's population: 16%

Economy: Wealthy, based on successful export of agricultural goods from fertile land.

Climate: Subtropical. Humid. Four seasons.

Average temperatures: 0–10 °C in winter, 21–32 °C in summer

Average annual rainfall: 1,500 mm

The Iguaçu falls are one of the natural wonders of the world consisting of a total of 275 waterfalls over a precipice 1.8 miles wide.

'I live here in Foz do Iguaçu and I cross the border every morning to work in my uncle's clothes shop in Paraguay. There are many other Lebanese people who have moved here and who run successful businesses.'
*– **Ahmed, an immigrant from Lebanon.***

POPULATION: MID-EUROPEAN INFLUENCE

The large number of Amerindian peoples who once lived in the south were greatly reduced by slave traders from Brazil and the Spanish colonies in Uruguay and Argentina. They were also affected by Jesuit missionaries, who rounded up men, women and children in order to convert them to Christianity in fortified villages.

The main influences on the population of the south today are the descendants of European and Middle Eastern immigrants. The fertile lands attracted large numbers of Germans, Italians, Poles, Russians, Syrians and Lebanese. In the extreme south, cowboys (*gauchos*), the descendants of Amerindian and European families, still work on the ranches.

SOCIAL CONDITIONS: HIGH STANDARDS OF LIVING

The south is economically successful and has the highest standard of living in Brazil. Cities like Curitiba are well ordered and show little of the poverty seen elsewhere. However, because of problems in other regions, there are large numbers of poor migrants heading to the south. *Favelas* are beginning to spring up around the main urban centres.

41

THE ECONOMY: BREADBASKET OF BRAZIL

The farms and ranches of the south are the leading wheat producers of Brazil. The state of Paraná has extensive plantations of pine trees and coffee bushes, whilst in Rio Grande do Sul, huge cattle herds wander across the pampas. Other important products are wine, timber, soya beans, potatoes and maté, a herbal tea. The region is also the largest producer of chicken and pork.

The south has a major leather industry, all of Brazil's coal reserves, and huge hydroelectric power potential. Increasing numbers of tourists visit the south of Brazil today; many come to see the spectacular Iguaçu Falls.

Brazilian Wine

The southern state of Rio Grande do Sul is responsible for 90 per cent of all the wine produced in Brazil. The main producers are the descendants of Italian immigrants. The temperate climate and the terrain are similar to those of southern Italy.

Today, the area has a distinct Italian atmosphere. In many wine cellars, salamis and cheeses hang from the ceilings. Brazilian wines were, for a long time, produced just for local consumption, but Brazil is planning to challenge Chile and Argentina and become South America's leading wine producer and exporter.

'Here at the Aurora Co-operative [wine producers] we believe that Brazil will rival Chile and Argentina in the next decade as South America's primary producer of fine wines.' –wine worker, Aurora Co-operative, Rio Grande do Sul.

The Italian immigrants who have settled in the state of Rio Grande do Sul have established a wine industry which produces 90 per cent of Brazil's wine output.

The dam of Itaipu, the world's largest hydroelectric power station. Although the dam means that more electricity can be produced, critics argue that it causes too much environmental damage.

ITAIPU DAM

Only 17 km north of the Iguaçu Falls is Itaipu, the world's largest hydroelectric power scheme. It is located on the mighty Paraná river, which forms a border with Paraguay. Work began on the dam in the early 1970s, but it was not until 1990 that all eighteen 700,000 kilowatt generators were brought into use, at a cost of US$25 billion.

Much of the money for this colossal scheme was borrowed from the World Bank, contributing to Brazil's already enormous debt. Those in favour of mega-projects such as this argue that the rapidly growing industries of the south and south-east need Itaipu's huge electrical capacity and that without it development would be slowed down.

Critics of the project claim that Brazil neither needs nor can afford such schemes, and that the nation would be better off with smaller ones, closer to the main centres of population.

Severe environmental and social problems have been caused by the dam and the creation of a 1350 km² reservoir. Some 40,000 families were forced off their land, with little or no compensation. The reservoir drowned thousands of animals and changed the local climate.

43

The future of Brazil

'Brazil is a paradise. We have a beautiful country with many natural riches.
– Eduardo, a taxi driver in Bauru.

Large families are common in Brazil. Today nearly half of all Brazilians are under 20 years of age. In the UK more than a fifth of the population is over 60.

Brazil is in many ways a very fortunate country. With its enormous natural resources and mineral wealth, there is great potential for economic development in the future. But the biggest challenge will be whether or not Brazil can develop socially as well, so that the majority of its population can enjoy a reasonable standard of living. To enable this to happen, the huge gap between rich and poor will have to be closed and land redistributed more fairly.

Brazilian politicians often blame their huge foreign debt – now the biggest of any developing country – for their inability to solve many of their problems. With a debt three times as large as export earnings each year, repayment is certainly a very difficult task. In the last thirty years, Brazil has had periods of rapid economic growth, but there has been a tendency towards large-scale projects which need huge investment to start them up. Smaller, less expensive schemes employing more people would help to spread benefits more widely.

In order to pay for expensive projects, government spending on social services has continually been cut. Many of the improvements made to people's lives have come about only because of the actions of local non-government organizations and charities.

Bad housing, lack of sanitation and poor diet are all factors contributing to the high death rate among infants. Children born to mothers who live in the *favelas* of the north-east, for example, are six times as likely to die of

The education system in Brazil is biased towards university students. For Brazil to progress socially more resources need to be used to increase the general education standards for everyone.

diarrhoea, serious respiratory infections and malnutrition as those whose mothers can afford to go to university.

Education needs to be drastically improved. At the moment, the government spends ninety times as much public money on educating 500,000 mostly well-off, university students as it does on providing a basic education for 30 million children. As many as 5 million children between the ages of 7 and 14 do not go to school at all.

As a nation, Brazilians have a great ability to compromise, even in the most difficult of situations. This is found not just in politics but in every walk of life. The expression *'dar um jeito'* means to find a solution or way out of a situation. Despite the widespread corruption and many delays, things do, in the end, get done. It remains to be seen whether Brazil can somehow find a fair way forward towards a society in which there is respect for all its people, and its environment, or whether it will keep to the model it has followed so far – of prosperity only for the few.

Glossary

Altitude tropical A tropical climate affected by the height of the land.

Civilian government A government elected by the people.

Colony A community formed by settlers in a country that is far from their homeland.

Commerce The buying and selling of goods and services.

Discrimination Treating people unfairly because of their race, colour, religion or sex.

Elite A small number of powerful people or organizations.

Equatorial climate A climate with high temperatures and rainfall all year round, shared by countries on or near the Equator.

Free trade zone An area in which national taxes don't apply.

Genocide Deliberately killing a whole group of people.

Human rights Basic rights laid down by international law which all people should be entitled to.

Hydroelectric schemes A group of structures designed to generate electricity by using the power of water.

Inaugurated Officially opened.

Inflation A general increase in prices.

Investment capital A large sum of money used to set up a business or industry.

Military government An unelected government made up of members of the armed forces.

Multinationals Large companies that have factories or offices in more than one country.

Per capita income The total wealth a country produces a year (Gross Domestic Product) divided by the number of people in that country.

Processing industries Industries that transform raw products into goods that can be sold.

Savannah Open grassland in the tropics or subtropics with few trees and bushes growing

Service sector The part of the economy which is involved in providing services rather than making goods.

Topographical zones Areas of similar physical geography.

Tropical climate A climate of constant high temperatures and rainfall found between the Tropics of Capricorn and Cancer.

Further information

Brazilian Embassy, 32 Green Street, London, W1Y 4AT, has a good library and can provide pamphlets for schools.

Brazil Network, PO Box 1325, London, SW9 6BG.

Hispanic and Luso-Brazilian Council, Education Department, Canning House, 2 Belgrave Square, London, SW1X 8PJ, has an excellent library on South America and can recommend sources of audiovisual material.

Living Earth Foundation, Warwick House, 106 Harrow Road, London W2 1XD, can provide publications for schools to help teach environmental issues.

Oxfam, Education Department, 274 Banbury Road, Oxford, OX2 7DZ, has a special education programme and produces publications, videos, slide-sets and leaflets.

Save the Children Fund, 17 Grove Lane, London SE5 8RD, can provide information on the plight of Brazil's children.

Survival International, 310 Edgware Road, London, W2 1DY, has up-to-date information on Brazil's Amerindian peoples and special material for children.

Books to read

Brazil: A Mask called Progress by Neil MacDonald (Oxfam, 1991)
Countries of the World: Brazil by Julia Waterlow (Wayland, 1992)
Country Fact File: Brazil by Marion Morrison (Simon and Schuster, 1993)
Insight Guides: Brazil edited by Edwin Taylor (APA Publications (HK) Ltd, 1992)
The Amazon Rainforest and its People by Marion Morrison (Wayland, 1993)
The World's Rivers: The Amazon by Julia Waterlow (Wayland, 1992)
Threatened Cultures: Rainforest Amerindians by Anna Lewington (Wayland, 1992)

Index

Numbers in **bold** refer to illustrations.